# Trying on the Night Sky

## Mary McCormack

Cover Photo & Design by Alyson Haas

ISBN: 978-0-9981720-6-4

## *Also by Mary McCormack*

*Tastes of Sunlight: Haiku for the Seasons*
*All the Words Kept Inside*
*Brushstrokes*
*Touching His Scar*

# Acknowledgments

Thank you, so much, to those friends and fellow writers who took the time to read my first drafts and offer feedback. You know who you are. I appreciate your insights, your encouragement, and your belief in me. The final product wouldn't have been the same without all of you.

Thank you to strangers, friends, and family alike who have reached out to say they were moved by my poetry.

Thank you to all of those who make me feel like what I do matters.

I'm honored to get the chance to share my writing. Thank you to *you*, reader, for choosing this book.

Also, thank you to the editors and judges of the following journals, contests, and anthologies in which current or earlier versions of these poems first appeared:

*cattails:* clear-running water
*Chrysanthemum:* clearing the birdbath
*failed haiku:* a flute lifted, heart on my sleeve, crème brûlée, my
    dress
*#FemkuMag:* negligee, something romantic
*first frost:* wild night
*Frogpond:* honey and violets, doors flung open, end of the road,
    twilight, rapture, vigil, the raven
*Haiku 2024:* inexperienced
*Haiku Girl Summer:* picnic weather, firefly, old French farmhouse,
    unknown to us, the cold, honeycomb light, if sunlight, that
    extra hesitation, sea breeze, deep in the forest
*Haiku Touchstone Award 2024 (Shortlisted):* inexperienced
*HSA Anthology 2023 and 2024:* dappled nap, collecting
*Kingfisher:* inexperienced, peeling the orange
*Mayfly:* shattering
*Modern Haiku:* a sliver of mint, the touch of cold water
*Presence:* if a dream, drifting, Raspberry Lane, mahogany
    handrail, snow on the handrails
*prune juice:* olive tray, hi!
*Shamrock Haiku:* a redbud's veins, grains of salt
*The Heron's Nest:* rowing a boat
*tsuri-dōrō:* shaking off, so perfect
*Under the Bashō:* clover flowers, watercolor painting
*upside down: The Red Moon Anthology of English-Language Haiku
    2023:* olive tray
*Vancouver Cherry Blossom Haiku Invitational 2024 (Sakura Award):*
    her aria
*Wales Haiku Journal:* morning chorus, climbing, sipping
    dewdrops, scent of the meadow, hush, lingering

# Trying on
# the Night Sky

*patchwork quilt*
*all the moments*
*that make a story*

*from stranger*
*to beloved…*
*the slow shift of seasons*

speckled egg
the path spotted
with pear tree petals


pre-fear
goslings wander
into the woods

a melody
washing over me
rays of light


morning chorus
I clear my throat
to join

daydreaming words in the creek's babble

pink pink pink peony

celebrating spring in my step

a
flute
lifted
to
my
lips
tipsy
on
cham-
pagne

olive tray
I pick
the lonely one

one world
passes another —
strangers



folded wings
a million questions
I keep to myself

lavender soap
the bathroom an oasis
from the party

can't sleep...
replaying
the way you said *hi*

midnight
a serenade
of frogs


lily pad to lily pad
following
my dream

pale pink dawn
I slip a dress
over my shoulders

the brush of bare feet
on cool floorboards
morning's first light

second story —
eye to eye
with a sparrow

a redbud's veins
magnified
by a dewdrop

clover flowers
strewn through dark grass —
so many stars


barefoot
more careful
where I step

muddy river bank
goslings scramble up
ahead of their parents


picnic weather
my date
with apricots

lilac blooms
licking the last bit of honey
from the spoon




deeper into the forest
I follow the doe
with my eyes

a dappled nap beneath linden leaves whispering

pointillism...
I study
the tips of grass

wind...
reading the pages of my journal
one by one by one

thoughts of you swimming from my pen seahorses

confidence rising tide


seeking
each other out...
chance meeting

hi!
hiya!
hyacinth!



impressionism
the yellow-blue dazzle
of seeing you

traipsing through mud
not a care in the world —
first date


*look!*
each petal
in the breeze

go go go stop
go go go stop
the robin

falling in
with the goslings
a baby blue jay

with a yawn
a tiny fairy opens
cobweb curtains




daybreak
cupped in the star magnolia
pure light

a tree
snags your hat
for itself

big enough
to be my umbrella
the sycamore leaf




orchard wall
we rest
against warm stone

a sheen of sweat
on your forearms…
meandering thoughts

deep blush
your eyes linger
on mine

slow
motion
falling
in
love
with
today

spring equinox
tilting my glass
to yours

the barest caress…
wind
on foxgloves

skittish
the touch of your voice
all I can handle


a soft breeze…
the way you ask
if I've been hurt

shattering into crystal clear insights

strong
until I'm not...
broken branch


hibiscus sunset...
the gentleness
of your hand on mine

river eddy —
that catch
in my throat


who notices
the fallen twig
far from all it's known?

parts of the past clinging onion skin

scrubbing at the stain
last to fade
its outline


your voice
embracing me…
deep blue night

water glass...
resting my lips
where yours were

falling asleep
to the sound
of my breathing

morning meditation
humming a tune
only I know

the duet
of grass
and dew

budding oaks...
the forest swathes me
in green


scent of the meadow
lingering in my hair
wild violets

spring thaw
what your eyes
reveal


something romantic
about this rain…
hawthorn woods

maiden voyage
my lips
to yours

a tulip's curve…
the beginning
of my smile

reverie…
the language
of strawberries and cream

my aria lifting into wind petals from a cherry tree

outdoor café
chairs swept aside
for dancing


my dress brushes against your imagination

shaking off
my jitters —
jitterbug

stepping stones…
one choice
to another




exactly when ready
a tulip opens
to the sun

our hug
lengthening
into desire




awakening…
a rose
from bud to bloom

watercolor
your kiss
spreads through me

honey and violets
a taste
of my imagination




delicate
the word itself
handled with care

rowing a boat
into the lake
into the sky

sun-soaked meadow…
eyes closed
our pinkies touch

a raven
trying on
a wren's voice

so soft
your fingertip
on the violet

the intimacy
before
the intimate

*hush…*
tiny white flowers
in bloom

at the top of the hill
then higher
strawberry moon




hand in hand
tipsy
on starlight

if a dream
could be a dress...
trying on the night sky

sudden shower
our laughter carried off
by the wind




stripping down
after the rain
body heat

silk sheets...
the promise
of a night together



a sliver of mint...
what the moon
might taste like

just out of the bath
droplets shimmer
in my curls




your eyes stripped naked desire

deeper and deeper
into the kiss we emerge
within each other

night sky…
you trace a blackberry
across my nakedness


breath trembling aspen leaves at the window

a firefly here and gone my epiphany

inexperienced moonlight in the bed of lilies

your moan becomes mine becomes yours

shy to look at you
before
and after

breaking daylight
you make breakfast
while I'm still asleep




exquisite lingering on the tongue

traveled the world
and a day
in that kiss




old French farmhouse
deep in lavender
a bumblebee

honeycombing my hair golden drops of water




rain on rocks
that glimmer
in your eyes

silence
opening an avenue
for sound




unknown
to us
the language of daisies

forest banquet
willow fronds lend green
to the goblets


in the hammock
relaxing…
a ladybug

midsummer maple
not even a hint
of what's to come




mirage…
a shimmer of blue
in the dragonfly's wings

watercolor painting the forest full of light

summer solstice
a fawn steps
across the path

deep in the forest
cottonwood fluffs drift
out of time

the cold
before the taste
watermelon

trying to give the bee
a wide berth...
it follows me

apricot
gelato
afternoon




twirling once
twice
a cottonwood fluff

at
walking

a gosling's pace
I pause

here
there...

parting branches
I follow an unknown path
through my thoughts


clear-running water
my shadow bathes
without me

gust of wind —
diving for napkins
we spill the sangria

nectarine tango

longest day
we don't wait
till dark

pink-orange glow…
you nudge the dress
off my shoulders




          your fingers on        lace
                    beneath

water lilies
how I bloom
in your hands


oh, the softness
    the *soft*ness
of this night

iris to iris
the confluence
of rivers


candlelight…
shy to speak
the words that come to me

unbuttoning your formality

slipping into bed clothed only in shadow

honeycomb light
we sleep
till midday


whistling
with no one around to hear…
the wind

climbing
all over the cottage
wild roses


if sunlight
had a voice...
goldfinch

cantaloupe summer
afternoons whiled away
kissing




doors flung open
the grand entrance
of wind

that extra hesitation
before stepping outside —
bikini




sea breeze
my nose leads me
to the beach

the ocean collecting every shade of blue




chocolate-covered cherries
savoring
        twilight

end of the road
a path
into fields of lavender

thunderstorm…
the back and forth of your thumb
across my knuckles

breath hitching
I let my thigh
touch yours

wild night
the sheets in a tangle
on the clothesline


waking
to the sound of rain...
a fading dream

touching
your cheek
a spiderweb trembles




long pauses
in our conversation
death of a loved one

lost to my sight
the butterfly emerges
in another's


lips to flute to notes
to air
this sorrow through us all

grains of salt
on my fingertips
catching light




a vee of geese
silent
through clouds

vigil...
the elm
in a circle of lost leaves

twilight deepens stained glass angels singing

lingering farewell
the scent of honeysuckle
fades into autumn



spiced cider…
choosing
a night in

autumn chill
tucking myself deeper
into the book

*Raspberry Lane*
I give myself a moment
with the words

sipping dewdrops…
the cool morning
enters me




clearing the birdbath
of leaves
another one settles in

stone-soft melody
my fingertips
play moss

gale-force wind
our hug
after only hours apart

drifting
into our conversation
a maple leaf


cold bench
I scoot
closer to you

your breath warming my hands in yours




autumn wind
whispering through birch leaves
the lightest kiss

early dusk…
your jacket
around my shoulders




inhaling the night full of stars

fall equinox…
the garden statues
throw a party



midnight breeze…
the slow dance
of mushrooms

where we once lay…
the shadows
of a silver poplar


across the dance floor floating lights

biting
through fig skin…
lovers' evening

autumn leaves
stirring
the artist in you

almost a caress
the final dab of paint
on the canvas

languid morning
I rest a while longer
in memories of last night


the whisper of leaves
we listen...
listen

in the bathtub
leaning back
against you

the rhythm
of bathwater
of breath

you kiss my toes
one by one
rustling leaves




the novels
we tell each other
with our eyes

just
taking
you
in
every
last
inch

rapture within the grape's light

autumn storm
my hair drenched
in leaves



lingering in the rain-soaked kiss

half astonished
half of course
*even the leaves love you*

your smile
brings mine
into being

heart on my sleeve
everyone
stares

the panic
of loving someone
so much

touching the river
without a sound
a leaf carries on

red currant wine
dreaming of all the places
I've never been



on the river
the leaf's stem
a prow

first taste of winter
a snowflake
lands on my nose




*crème brûlée*
on my tongue
those syllables

negligee
as if dressed
in moonlight


the flare
of silence
between us

intertwined branches …
finding ourselves
in each other



abstract
art
lines
becoming

whispering
into the wee hours
snow

raspberries
in a white bowl
winter dawn

ivy
notebook
my
of
side
the
up
twining
sketch
a

the touch of cold water...
I rinse the leeks
long after the sand is gone

sipping eggnog
in silence…
snowfall

mahogany handrail
I linger on the stairs
before greeting guests

fir tree under snow
the house party
from outside


slow dance
a snowflake twirls
with the night

crackling fire…
I nestle
into you


half in half out
of sleep…
winter solstice

sunrise
the taste of butter, still cold
on baked bread

                    peeling the orange a cathedral

in the garden
a small sculpture
of our kiss


the robin's head, too,
turns...
snowflake landing

slant of sunlight
on the pillow
an invitation

those wandering goslings
turn up
in my dream

your quiet song
drifting upstairs
the scent of cinnamon



evening shadows...
the comfort
of your leg over mine

falling asleep to the scratch of your pencil wakes me


from wild onion
to ballroom gown —
the artist's touch

orange-blossom tea
everything else can wait
till tomorrow

snowstorm…
pirouettes land
without a sound

frosted window...
adding a fingerprint
to the patterns




each chimney
a palace turret...
snowfall

ice moon
the garden gate
frozen shut


snowshoe hare…
the silence
of footprints

snow on the handrails
we descend
to the blue-black river


not until
we're next to them —
deer

sunset unraveling a thread of orange

watercolor
letting the shapes
discover themselves

a tint of green
in my hair
pine needles




a long sigh
at the end of the day
unhooking my bra

constellations gleaming across my skin your kisses

starlight
the dance begins
with our eyes

*Chopin*
as our lips touch
snowflakes

so perfect
I'm afraid
of the last note

in a song

a century

no choreography
we begin
to waltz


that soft exhale…
finding myself
home at last

the epiphany
keeps unfolding…
us

## About the Author

Mary McCormack, award-winning writer, is a teacher
of poetry, fiction, and nonfiction. Her work is widely
published in the US and internationally.

www.marymwriter.com